Walks on High Dartmoor

Paul White

Bossiney Books · Launceston

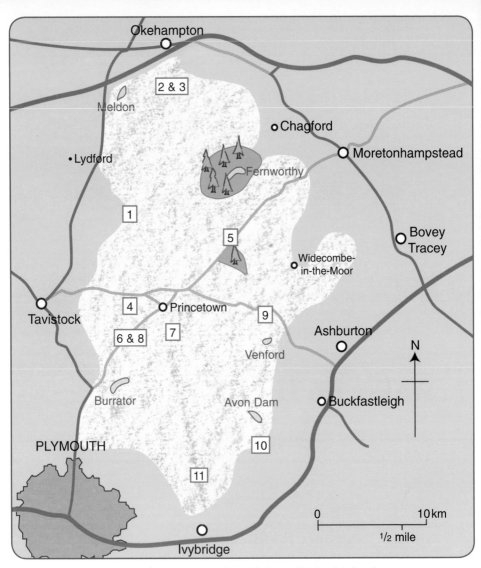

The starting points of the walks in this book

First published 2010
Bossiney Books Ltd, Langore, Launceston, Cornwall PL15 8LD
www.bossineybooks.com

ISBN 978-1906474-17-1

Acknowledgements
The maps are by Nick Hawken. All photographs are by the author.
Printed in Great Britain by R Booth Ltd, Penryn, Cornwall

Introduction

These walks have been carefully chosen to enable you to see some of the wildest and most dramatic scenery of Dartmoor – but with ease of walking, ease of navigation and peace of mind. They vary in length from 7.25 to 20km (4¹/₂ to 12¹/₂ miles) but make full use of former railways, leats and vehicle tracks, so there are few steep gradients. You can even climb Devon's two 'mountains' without much effort!

Safety

I don't want to be over-dramatic, but high Dartmoor can be tricky, even dangerous. If you are safety conscious, you will probably have no problems, but you definitely need to go prepared. Some of these walks will take you into lonely places where mobile phones get no reception so getting help is not always straightforward. Don't walk alone, and always make sure someone knows where you are going and when you expect to get back.

Weather is the most obvious danger. It can change abruptly, and the hills can suddenly be shrouded in cloud. It is then vital to know just where you are. This is one of the reasons why I have made such extensive use of leats and tracks: they are relatively easy to follow in fog.

As a precaution, you need to have a proper map with you, such as the Ordnance Survey sheet OL28 (the sketch maps in this book may be adequate for normal walking, but would be of little use if you lost your bearings) as well as a compass and/or a GPS if you have one. I confess I am something of a fair weather walker, and pay a lot of attention to the BBC's on-line local weather forecast.

As for snow and ice, unless you are an experienced hill walker please don't risk it. (I have found ice a particular problem on Dartmoor's steep tarmac lanes: it can be impossible to stand up, let alone walk!)

Equipment

The high moor will always be colder than the lowlands, and wind chill is often a factor. In fog the temperature drops abruptly. You should always carry extra layers of clothing in your rucksack as well as waterproofs. A hat and gloves can come in useful (sunhat in summer). You should carry a good supply of water with you, because dehydration makes you tired. My rucksack also includes torch, whistle, miniature penknife and a first aid kit: as yet I have had no need of them, but maybe tomorrow...

Good boots (and good walking socks) are vital for grip and ankle support: turning an ankle is all too easy where the ground is uneven, or obscured by bracken. Don't be surprised if the ground is squelchy in places, particularly in valley bottoms, even in summer. Some of the walks involve crossing streams which were small when I walked the routes: be very cautious if you find them swollen after rain or melting snow. In such conditions, the larger rivers can be deadly.

Many walkers, myself included, find a walking pole a useful accessory, not least for testing boggy ground.

Most of these walks have neither refreshment nor toilet facilities en route (walks 6 and 7 are the exceptions).

The military ranges

There is one further hazard after the weather and the mires – the military ranges which cover a large part of the north-west moor. When there is live firing, huge red flags are flown on the hilltops. All the ranges are generally open to the public at weekends – though Willsworthy Range (Walk 1) is closed on the weekend which includes the second Sunday in the month – and all are open on bank holidays and in August. But the Okehampton Range (Walks 2-3) is open for much of the summer – in the year of writing, for the whole of April, May, June, August and half of September.

Google 'Dartmoor ranges' or phone 0800 458 4868 to get up-to-date information on when the ranges are open.

Medieval clapper and 18th century turnpike bridges at Postbridge

In the unlikely event of finding military debris while out walking, needless to say, don't touch it! Take a note of its position and report it.

Much of the high moor is used for open grazing, by cattle, sheep and ponies. Please respect the needs of those whose livelihood depends on the moor: steer clear of the animals, don't feed the ponies, keep dogs under control, close gates as appropriate.

And finally the most important instruction of all: enjoy the walks!

What you will see

There have been three periods of intensive activity on Dartmoor, during which improving climate or population pressures made this marginal land more attractive. The altitude at which people were prepared to farm has varied over time, with the highest settlements being abandoned as the climate worsened and the moorland then used only for summer grazing.

Abandonment of the high ground helped preserve structures which could well have been ploughed out, or raided for useful stone, if they had been in the middle of highly populated farmland.

The three periods of intense activity were (dates approximate):

2000-800BC – the Bronze Age, when Dartmoor weather was quite benign. Some 5000 'hut circles' survive, many of them at slightly lower altitudes, as well as numerous ceremonial sites. Several walks in this book feature stone rows.

AD1000-1350 – the high Middle Ages, when population growth caused people to recolonise the moor, until the Black Death thinned them out and removed the need to do so. Apart from wayside and boundary crosses, several clapper bridges and two 'pounds' which were used for corralling livestock, there is little obvious evidence for this period on these particular walks.

1750-1900 – the early modern period, when over-optimistic agricultural improvers thought they could conquer nature, and industrialists saw opportunities in the extractive industries (tin and other ores, china clay and granite, as well as peat).

For more detailed information on the Bronze Age and the medieval period, please see *Ancient Dartmoor* and *Medieval Dartmoor*, both by Paul White and published by Bossiney Books.

Certainly in the Middle Ages and the modern period, and quite possibly in the Bronze Age, agriculture was accompanied by tin extraction. You will see, especially in valley bottoms, many examples of uneven ground ('turmoiled ground' in the delightful phrase of a contemporary of Shakespeare) which are the result of digging and sieving in search of ore.

This mining activity was powered by water wheels, and they in turn were served by leats – artificial water channels which run along the contours of many hills, some still carrying water but many now dry because they have not been maintained.

Granite, or 'moorstone', has been used for local construction purposes for 4000 years. The source was originally the loose stones or clitter left lying on the surface as a result of natural weathering. Commercial quarries only began around 1800, and depended on new transport infrastructure – roads and railways – to remove the stone.

Several of the walks make use of disused railway tracks, including the Plymouth & Dartmoor Railway, originally a horsedrawn line which had reached King Tor quarry by 1823. In 1883 it became the Princetown Railway, carrying tourists as well as granite, but it never achieved profitability, finally closing in 1956.

The Redlake Mineral Railway, which now makes such a splendid access into the moor for walkers, was not built until 1911. It served the china clay works at Redlake, carrying coal and workers to the pit: the clay itself flowed down in liquid form through a pipe. The clay had been worked out by 1932.

Foggintor Quarry (see Walk 4), formerly known as Royal Oak Quarry, dates back at least to 1820, but it may have been worked on a smaller scale well before that; production ceased around 1900

Leats had been used to supply water to towns from the 16th century, but the scale of the water industry changed in 1898 with the completion of Burrator Reservoir. The Avon reservoir was not finished till 1959, and Meldon reservoir only in 1972. One water industry feature you will notice on the high moor is lines of stone boundary posts – not to be confused with prehistoric stone rows! – defining catchment areas, for example PCWW or Plymouth City Water Works.

Forestry began to afflict the moor only after WW1, when the Forestry Commission was required to create a strategic timber reserve. The conifer plantations remain intrusive, and from time to time great swathes are felled, leaving a scene of devastation.

Military use of the moor started on a small scale during the Napoleonic Wars, but Okehampton Camp dates from 1875. Its continued use provokes a variety of strong feelings locally.

And there is one further activity which makes a major impact on the moor – leisure use both by local people and tourists. If you walk several of these routes you will soon see that there are a few 'hotspots' such as the path south from Princetown, and the summit of Yes Tor, but for the most part it is still easy to seek out wild and lonely places.

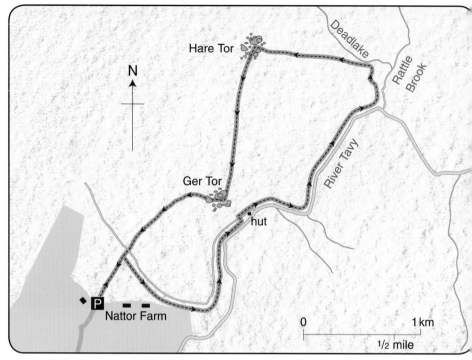

Walk 1 Tavy Cleave

Distance: 7.3km (4½ miles) Time: 3 hours

Character: A mere 7.3km, but probably the most strenuous walk in this book, heartily recommended to the fit and agile because of its dramatic scenery. After a gentle stroll beside a leat into the steep-sided Cleave, it becomes a scramble over and around boulders to avoid squelchy areas. Then a slow steady climb leads to two attractive tors with extensive views.

Access: This walk lies within the Willsworthy military range and access is limited. Normally it is open at weekends (but not the weekend containing the second Sunday in the month) and also on bank holidays and throughout August.

Check on www.dartmoor-ranges.co.uk or by the Freephone service on 0800 458 4868. Red flags are flown during live firing.

Safety: Do not attempt this walk if the river is running high. Do not touch any military debris you may find!

To get there: From Mary Tavy, follow the brown signs for the Elephant's Nest pub at Horndon, then follow signs for WILLSWORTHY and then LANE END. There is a car park at SX537823.

From the car park, head north-east towards Ger Tor. When you reach a leat with a gated crossing, turn right along the near bank, and follow it as it winds into the valley. At a small stone hut, cross the leat and pick your way up the valley with the river on your right. The path is uneven, and disappears entirely in places, so it's tough going but at least you can't get lost.

You will cross two minor streams, then after what may seem a long time will reach a confluence. Turn left, up the near bank of the Rattle Brook. Ascend the bank to avoid the damp patches. After 250 m the valley broadens out – this is 'Dead Lake Foot'. Turn left here, up a narrow dry valley heading roughly west. At the top, there is a broad path of sorts which heads steadily upward to the summit of Hare Tor (531 m).

Descend from the summit of the tor and head southwards on a grassy path towards Ger Tor which is at a lower level. From Ger Tor, pick your way down the scree-covered slope to the south-west of the tor, and head for the gated crossing over the leat, then back to the car park.

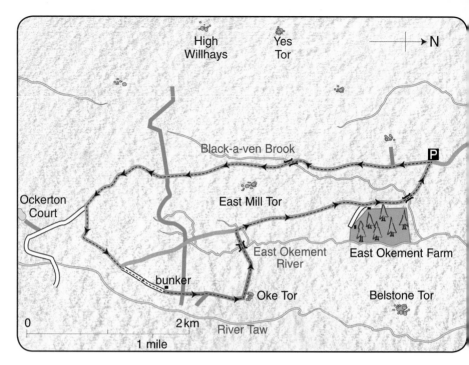

Walk 2   Okement Hill and Oke Tor

Distance: 11.5km (7 miles)   Time: 3 hours

Character: Majestic scenery approaching Devon's central watershed, a blanket bog at the heart of the northern moor where the rivers Taw, Dart and Okement rise within a few metres of each other. Much of the walk is on a potholed tarmac track, so you won't get lost or swallowed by the bog! A good option after wet weather – but choose a clear day.

Access: The walk is within the Okehampton Range (see page 4). Check before you go that the range is open.

To get there: From Okehampton follow signs for OKEHAMPTON CAMP. *Keep to the left when you reach the camp, cross a cattle grid and stream and continue climbing the tarmac track till you reach a large parking area on the right at a fork in the road (SX596922).*

From the fork, take the right branch. After 500m keep left, heading south. Cross New Bridge and continue heading south on the tarmac, climbing gently to the top of Okement Hill, bearing left past a military bunker.

(You might want to follow the rough track straight ahead, and then bear right on an old blocked track to Ockerton Court – where there

is a pool, and a ruin which might perhaps once have been a barn or a longhouse. But do not be tempted to continue south towards the famous but unimpressive Cranmere Pool. The ground is boggy and uneven, and the navigation confusing.)

From the bunker at the top of Okement Hill continue along the tarmac track, downhill. At a junction, bear right on a rough track uphill. When the track ends at another bunker, bear left heading north along the ridge, where a path leads towards Oke Tor.

From the tor head west to cross the stream by a bridge. On reaching the tarmac track, turn right and follow it past East Okement Farm, down over a stream and back to the car park.

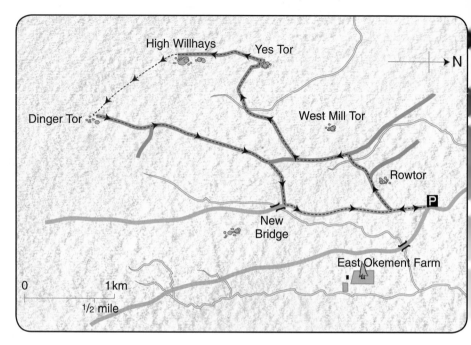

Walk 3 Yes Tor and High Willhays

Distance: 11km (6³/₄ miles)   Time: 3 hours
Character: Considering that this walk includes two 'mountains' (a British mountain is defined as over 610m high) this is a fairly easy walk, with straightforward navigation – mostly on or beside rough tracks. And it starts at an altitude of 417m, which helps! Choose a clear day.

Access: The walk is within the Okehampton Range (see page 4). Check before you go that the range is open.

To get there: As for walk 2.

From the fork by the car park, take the right branch, heading south. After 500m bear right on a rough track. This climbs, passes military structures, then crosses a stream. Immediately beyond the stream turn left at a T-junction.

After 600m, bear right at a fork, uphill. After winding a bit the modern military track ends. Turn right, up to the flagpole on Yes Tor (618m). This feels like the highest point on Dartmoor, but the surveyors insist High Willhays, which you can see to the south, is higher, at 621m. (If you can't see it because of mist, it may be best to retrace your steps rather than continuing the walk.)

12

Walk along the ridge to High Willhays, and continue to a small conical tor at the end of the ridge.

From this conical tor, take a beaten path heading south-east (more precisely, 145°) towards Dinger Tor – only just visible from this angle, merely a couple of rocky outcrops. The path may be faint at some times of year, and compared to the hard tracks it may seem spongy underfoot. Pass a boundary stone about 20 m to your right.

From Dinger Tor, turn left along the military track, heading north. Keep left at a fork. After 1.4 km, at the next junction turn right. The track winds downhill. On reaching a tarmac track – with notable pot-holes – turn left along it and it will take you back to the car park.

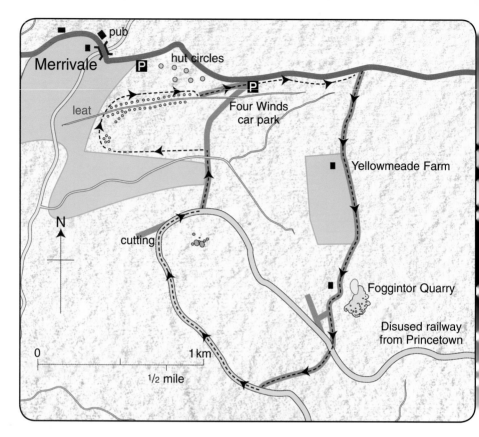

Walk 4   Foggintor and Merrivale

Distance: 7.25 km (4¹/₂ miles)   Time: 2 hours
Character: A walk with much of interest, and some glorious views:
generally easy walking except for what can be a very damp crossing of
a streambed which may also require a degree of agility.

Park at the Four Winds car park on the B3357 between The Dartmoor
Inn and the Princetown turn. This car park is distinguished by trees
and a rectangular stone enclosure, and was (improbable as this may
seem) the Foggintor School from 1915 to 1936, though it had been the
Walkhampton Foggintor Mission School before that.

Turn right out of the car park and walk up parallel to the road. At
the next car park, turn right on the access track towards Yellowmeade
Farm. Keep left at a fork to walk behind the back of the farm. You will
then pass on your left the entrance to the Foggintor Quarry, which
now includes a small lake. Continue ahead on the rough track which

14

winds through the quarry complex till you reach the point where it crosses the trackbed of the old Princetown railway, at what was once King Tor Halt.

Cross straight over and descend a rough track till you again reach the railway trackbed, which has looped around the hill. A favourite game for young Princetown men was to leave the train at King Tor and hare down the track to catch it when it stopped again at Ingra Tor. The really fit could manage this feat on the return journey!

Turn right when you reach the trackbed and follow it as it rises, gently for a walker but very steeply by railway standards, with splendid views across towards the hills of Cornwall, then of Vixen Tor and the tors of north Dartmoor. The track curves right through a cutting, and the view suddenly changes. At first there is a steep drop on the left. Once Yellowmeade Farm lies ahead of you, look for a path which diverges to the left, heading for the far right corner of a wall.

Cross the valley floor and the stream. Climb the bank and turn left along the top, as far as a standing stone, then bear right to pass the left side of a stone circle. Continue in the same direction to a pair of stones at the west end of a double stone row. (You may want to explore the parallel double row, and the hut circles near the line of the road.)

Walk up the row and at the top divert slightly right to the guide stone of an ancient trackway – the T and A stand for Tavistock and Ashburton. Then head back to the Four Winds car park.

15

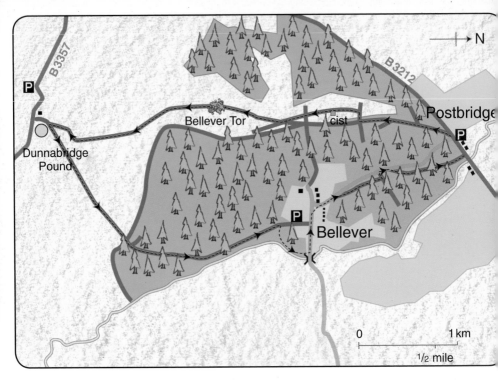

Walk 5   Postbridge, Bellever and Dunnabridge Pound

Distance: 10.5 km (6½ miles)   Time: 3 hours
Character: A mixture of attractive woodland, open moorland and
Bellever Tor with panoramic views over most of Dartmoor. Fairly easy
walking throughout.

Park at Postbridge, in the large car park. Turn right out of the car park
up the road for 100 m, then turn left (BELLEVER) and immediately turn
right into the forest. Bear left through a gate, PUBLIC FOOTPATH.

Ignore side turns. After 600 m, keep right at a fork. When the track
levels out, it is crossed by another track: turn right along it. After
180 m bear left, passing a grove of small deciduous trees on your right.
At the end of the grove, divert briefly left to a fenced area containing a
burial cist and stone row. (There are other prehistoric burial features
on this hilltop, but you will do well to spot them.)

Return to your previous course and follow the path towards Bellever
Tor, aiming initially towards the trees on the slope to the left. At a path
junction, bear right on the broad grassy path up to the summit, with
its extensive views. Then continue down the far side of the tor, to join
a clear but narrower path running almost due south.

Descend towards a ladder stile. Don't cross the stile, but turn left through a gate and continue with the wall on your right.

After a further gate, a fingerpost (PATH) guides you to cut the corner of the field, but then regain the wall on your right. At the bottom of the enclosure you will find a gate, with a track leading down to it. First take a look over the wall ahead into Dunnabridge Pound, then turn left up the track, which leads in a remarkably straight line through several gates.

Enter the forest, keeping right downhill at the first junction and following signs for BELLEVER. The track leads through a farmyard and then fields, before becoming again a forestry track. After a while the East Dart River suddenly comes into view.

Bear right through a gate and after 100m (just before the car park and toilets for this popular picnic spot) turn right to walk along the riverbank. Immediately before the road bridge are the remains of its medieval predecessor.

Turn left along the road, then opposite the car park access road bear right across a field, then turn right onto the lane. Climb the lane for 150m then bear right on a path which runs roughly parallel to the lane. At the top of the slope cross a farm access track, join the lane for 100m to avoid a boggy patch, then rejoin the grassy path now about 50m from the road.

Above: One of the ubiquitous Dartmoor ponies

Below: The Bellever Bridge area is a popular picnic site

Ignore side turnings and continue ahead towards a distant farm with twin gables. The path descends towards Postbridge. Turn left on the main road, back to the car park.

Walk 6 Devonport Leat and Princetown Railway

Distance: 17km (10 1/2 miles)   Time: 4 1/4 hours
Character: High moorland scenery, some of it lonely, but very easy
walking and navigation. One steep ascent. You could start from
Princetown, but we preferred to arrive there in time for lunch!

Start (as in Walk 8) from a pair of adjacent car parks on the north side
of the Yelverton to Princetown road, B3212 (SX560709).

Walk beside the road in the direction of Princetown. Just before the
road swings left, take the path bearing off to the right, towards the top
left corner of a conifer plantation. Then keep the wall of the plantation
on your right and descend till you cross the Devonport Leat.

Turn left along the bank of the leat. You will reach 'the Iron Bridge'
where the leat crosses the river. You could make a diversion from this
point – see next page.

> ### The Devonport Leat
>
> This is an artificial watercourse built in the 1790s to take fresh
> water to the fast-expanding dockyard area of Plymouth. It now
> feeds into Burrator reservoir.

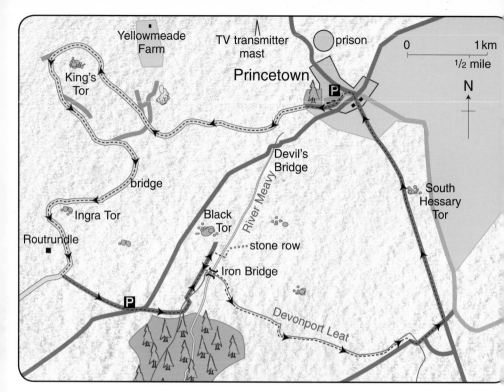

Cross the bridge on the north side, climb the steep rocky hill beside the tumbling water then cross the leat and follow its southern side for nearly 3 km.

Shortly after a granite block repair to the embankment, then a pond on the left, bear right down a path to join a stony track. Cross a stream then cross the leat. Keep left at a path junction and follow the stony track roughly north-east. When you reach a cross-track at a boundary stone (PCWW 1917) turn left. This very popular track will take you into Princetown.

The diversion (an additional 1.2 km)

Continue ahead along the bank of the river. You will see the remains of much industrial activity. Just below a waterfall are two blowing houses where tin was smelted, the bellows powered by waterwheels. Continue to a point above the waterfall, where a metal plank provides an apparently hazardous crossing. About 100 m further upstream on the far side of the river is a well-preserved stone row. Now return to the Iron Bridge and turn left.

Go forward at the roundabout then turn left at the war memorial, past the car park and the fire station. Bear left on a path, DISUSED RAILWAY, which leads you round a private area and to the railway trackbed.

Where a track from the quarry on the right crosses the trackbed, you could take a shortcut downhill – see map. Otherwise continue on the old railway, keeping left when it forks. Follow it round the next tor and keep left through a cutting. After going under a bridge and rounding Ingra Tor, you will see Routrundle farm on your right.

Just beyond it, turn left up a grassy track which leads from Routrundle and up to the car parks from which you started.

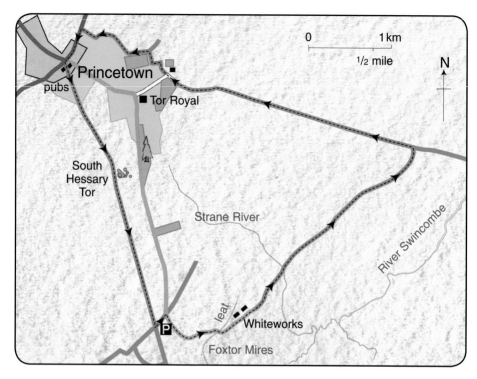

Walk 7 Whiteworks, Royal Hill and Princetown

Distance: 11.3km (7 miles)   Time: 2³/4 hours
Character: Fairly easy walking, though a stream crossing requires
either a degree of agility or wet feet. Can be spongy underfoot after
heavy rain.

The walk could be started from Princetown, but we started from near
Whiteworks in order to reach Princetown with its pubs and cafés at
lunchtime. Follow TOR ROYAL LANE from Princetown. When after
3 km (a couple of miles) the lane starts to bend left and down towards
Whiteworks, there are two parking places on the right.

Continue down the lane on foot, crossing the Devonport Leat
and passing a row of cottages – all that remains of this once thriving
mining community, except for ruins. To your right is Foxtor Mire or
Mires, the serious bog which inspired Conan Doyle's 'Great Grimpen
Mire' in *The Hound of the Baskervilles.*

When the tarmac ends, continue ahead on PUBLIC BRIDLEWAY
through industrial ruins to a gate. There is then a clear grassy track.
When it divides, most walkers will choose the right fork with a short

leap across a stream but if you are wearing wellies, the left fork may be easier! There is further soft ground beyond the ford, then a hill, then a descent to another boggy stream crossing: a little to the right of centre is probably best.

Not long after this the path approaches a field wall and a path junction. Turn left up a broad track, BRIDLEPATH PRINCETOWN, which aims slightly to the left of the TV transmitter mast. In time the path becomes a rough track, and ultimately descends to a gate.

Follow the concrete drive for 50 m then turn right, PATH. At a path junction, turn left, PUBLIC BRIDLEWAY TO PRINCETOWN. Cross a leat and continue uphill on a rough track, which winds into Princetown.

Turn left at the road, then at the mini-roundabout turn left between the two pubs. A well walked and well surfaced path leads onto the moor, passing South Hessary Tor. You will see a series of boundary stones. When you reach a track crossing with a boundary stone *on the right* (PCWW 1917), turn left, which will take you back to your starting point.

Whiteworks was one of the larger tin mines but worked only inter-mittently, between 1820 and 1876 – exact dates are hard to establish. The scale of the operation is still very evident on the ground.

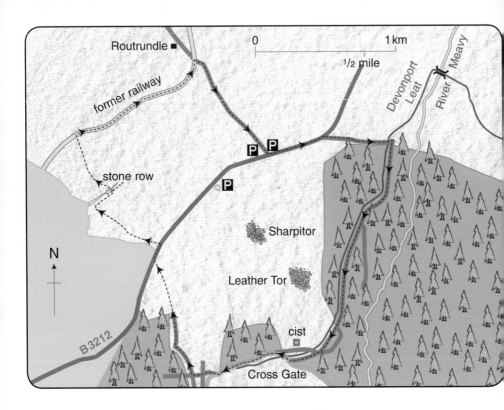

Walk 8 Around Sharpitor

Distance: 7.25km (4¹/₂ miles) Time: 2 hours
Character: A mixture of attractive woodland and open moorland,
with some extensive views. There is one long steep ascent of about 85m
(altitude, not distance!) but otherwise this is an easy walk.

Start from a pair of adjacent car parks on the north side of the
Yelverton to Princetown road, B3212 (SX560709). Walk beside the
road in the direction of Princetown.

Just before the road swings left, take the path bearing off to the
right, towards the top left corner of a conifer plantation. Then keep
the wall of the plantation on your right and descend till you cross the
Devonport Leat, an artificial watercourse built in the 1790s to take
fresh water to the fast-expanding dockyard area of Plymouth.

Cross the leat and turn right, PUBLIC FOOTPATH CROSSGATE AND
YENNADON. Keep the leat on your right, ignoring turnings to the left.
This will lead you to Cross Gate – note the medieval cross on your
left. (Just before Cross Gate, where a broad track crosses the leat-side

path, you could divert along the track on the far side of the leat to see the remains of a burial mound and cist.)

Join a quiet lane and continue ahead, ignoring stiles on the right, for about 500 m. When the lane bends slightly left and downhill, bear right and follow a waymarked footpath. At a footpath crossing, immediately before a forestry plantation, turn right uphill – unsigned, but a well used path. Climb steeply with the woodland on your left. When you finally reach the end of the plantation, continue ahead in the same northerly direction and you will reach a road.

Cross the road and turn right along the verge. At the end of the wall and fence turn left and head north-west, roughly parallel to the enclosures on your left. When you reach a boggy stream, turn right up it, both for an easier crossing point and to see a stone row built alongside the stream.

Now cross the stream and head north or north-west – easily done when the bracken is down, but in summer you will need to find whatever paths head in that direction. There are old pits and other hazards here, so don't just charge through the bracken! You will reach a disused railway line. Turn right along it.

After 1 km the track swings sharply (by railway standards) to the left. It is crossed by an old track from Routrundle farm. Turn right up this track, which leads back to the twin car parks.

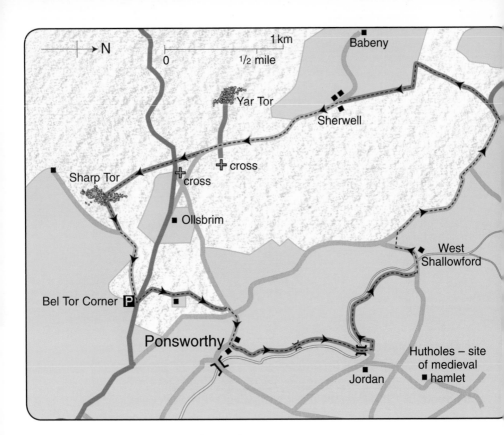

Walk 9 Ponsworthy and Yartor Down

Distance: 10.6km (6½ miles)   Time: 3 hours
*Character: Initially there is a reminder of the gentler aspects of the
moor, with delightful woodland and thatched cottages, then a steady
climb to high moorland, ending with a glorious view over the wooded
Dart valley from Sharp Tor. Some uneven walking, and likely to be
squelchy in places.*

Park at the Bel Tor Corner car park (SX695731). Cross the road and
follow the path opposite, downhill and northward, through a pattern
of 'reaves'. These are the remains of a 3000 hectare (12 square mile)
field system, laid out in perfect parallel lines around 1800 years before
the arrival of the Romans.

Keep left of the Primm Cottage enclosure, then bear right along the
enclosure wall, and continue ahead in the same direction along a path
or track. On reaching a lane, turn right, go forward at the cross roads
and descend steeply to Ponsworthy.

Just before a shallow ford, turn left on a footpath (JORDAN), which leads through a wood beside a stream. After 1.2 km a footbridge takes you into Jordan, where you need to turn left on the bridleway.

However, it's worth making a 200 m diversion to the right to see the lovely thatched manor house. A longer diversion would take you to one of Dartmoor's best kept secrets, Hutholes – a late Saxon settlement abandoned around the time of the Black Death.

From Jordan PUBLIC BRIDLEWAY WEST SHALLOWFORD follows the river bank as far as a lane. Turn left. After 200 m, leave the lane and climb with the wall on your right to another lane. Turn right and follow the lane uphill.

About 400 m after passing a tarmac farm access track on the right, turn left on a metalled track (yellow waymark) and then bear left on a grassy track (yellow waymark). When you reach a wall, turn left and climb to the top of the enclosure, then turn right. Follow the track when it diverges from the wall, and heads for Shirwell. Turn left here along the lane, which begins a long ascent.

When the lane swings left at the top of the slope, continue ahead on a beaten path towards Sharp Tor. Cross the road, and continue to the tor, where there are views over the Dart Valley, Venford Reservoir and a large swathe of the moor. From the tor, head east down to join a lane, which leads back to the car park.

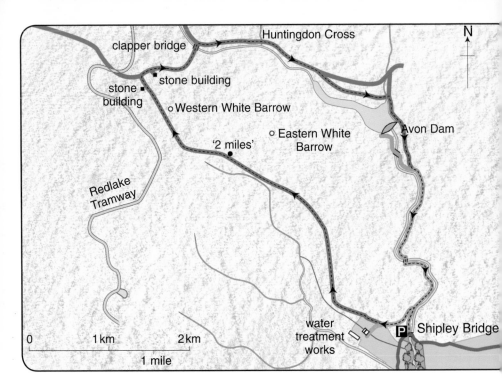

Walk 10   Shipley Bridge and Huntingdon Cross

Distance: 12km (7¹/₂ miles)   Time: 3¹/₂ hours
Character: A slightly more adventurous walk than many in this book,
reaching almost to the centre of the southern moor by using the route
of the former Zeal Tor horse-drawn tramway. It had wooden rails set
on granite blocks, so there is no smooth trackbed. The section of the
walk from the clapper bridge to Huntingdon Cross could be difficult
after heavy rain, and there are a couple of fords where you will get
your feet wet. This walk could be a bad option after a wet spell. Walk
11 is a longer but perhaps less demanding alternative.

Park at Shipley Bridge (SX 680629). Head north from the car park on a
tarmac track, with the river on your right. After 200m turn sharp left,
up another tarmac track, which climbs to a cattle grid. About 50m
before the cattle grid, divert right on a path which runs north of the
waterworks enclosure. Find a way through the gorse bushes, aiming
for the far top corner of the enclosure.

Here you will find a briefly embanked section of the old tramway,
and very soon it becomes an obvious path, climbing gently but inexo-

rably. After about 4 km, you will see to your right the Western White Barrow – a prehistoric cairn: unfortunately ruined by peat cutters who built a house within it in 1847.

Continue northward along the tramway past a stone structure and some old diggings to a very obvious track crossroads. Turn right here along the Abbots Way (now part of the Two Moors Way) and follow the well-walked path, which heads down to a clapper bridge. Cross the Avon here, and turn right along the bank, if conditions permit. (There are parallel paths higher up the slope if need be.) The riverside path leads to a gate. Cross the stile nearby, and to your left you will see the medieval waymark, Huntingdon Cross.

Continue by fording the stream, then turning right along the bank on a well-trodden path. At a fork, keep right on the easier path, which has good views over the reservoir. Cross a stream which feeds the reservoir and then scale the bank opposite. Turn right along the bank, to the dam.

From the dam a metalled track leads down (past a prehistoric settlement, but it's covered in bracken for much of the year) to the main tarmac access road, which leads through park-like scenery and past industrial remains to Shipley Bridge.

You might even find an ice-cream van waiting to tempt you.

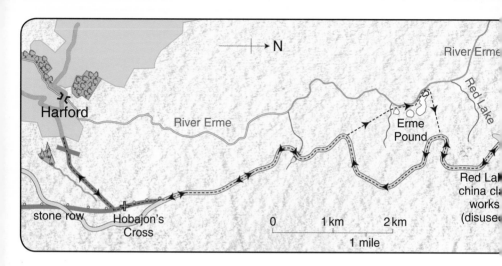

Walk 11 Erme Pound and Red Lake

Distance: 20.6km (12³/₄ miles) but could be cut to 17km
Time: 5 hours
*Character: Basically a there-and-back walk, but a great way to reach
the heart of the southern moor with minimal navigation and, most
unusually for southern England, not a single house is in sight the
whole way! Features include one very visible stone row and two Bronze
Age settlements, as well as the disused china clay works at the head
of the Redlake Tramway. Dramatic scenery in the Erme valley, then
rather desolate towards Red Lake – choose a cheerful sunny day.
Mostly easy walking. Compass and map necessary.*

Park at Harford Moor Gate (SX 643596), more easily approached from
Ivybridge rather than Cornwood. From the north side of the gated car
park head just north of east, on a bearing of about 80°, and continue
as far as possible on that bearing. The idea is to cross the valley which
is on your right, but at its head rather than its soggy centre, and then
to aim for the lowest point of the ridge ahead of you. Be sure to make
a mental note of the landmarks, which will be useful when you come
to retrace your steps.

Just before the top of the ridge you will meet a stone row – the
second longest on the moor at 2 km – with a path beside it. Turn left
along the path and continue past Hobajon's Cross (now just a cross
incised on a prehistoric stone, but a substantial monument in the
Middle Ages) and a curiously shaped standing stone, until the path is
joined by the trackbed of the Redlake Mineral Railway.

30

Continue in the same direction along the trackbed for nearly 4 km, until a point where the trackbed swings to the right revealing a view over the upper Erme, and there is an earthwork on the left at right-angles to the track. A faint path now diverts northward towards the distant river. It leads down to cross a stream (some agility or wet feet required). From the stream crossing, bear left.

Go through the wall of a Bronze Age pound, past massive stones which seem to have formed a very small hut, and out at the far side. The living accommodation was a hut to the north of the pound. Turn right on a path parallel with the river. This leads to the substantial walls of Erme Pound, a complex multi-phase structure. The main walls are actually a medieval re-build. Watch your footing as you explore it: this is no place to twist your ankle.

From the north end of Erme Pound, head east, uphill, over open tussocky grassland. You will be glad to regain the railway trackbed. Turn left if you wish to visit the disused Red Lake clay pit. Its spoil heap soon appears in the distance looking like a volcano on the far side of Red Lake Mire – 'lake' being a Devon dialect word meaning 'stream'.

Now return along the trackbed, and retrace your steps back to Harford.

Other Dartmoor walks books from Bossiney

There is no significant overlap between the walks in this book and three of our other Dartmoor walks books:

North Dartmoor Pub Walks (8-13km)
South Dartmoor Pub Walks (7-12km)
Shortish walks on Dartmoor (6-8km)

Shortish Walks on Dartmoor is strong on places of interest to walk to, particularly the antiquities. There are also two books of short walks:

Really Short Walks North Dartmoor (3-5km)
Really Short Walks South Dartmoor (3-5km)

And beyond Dartmoor...

North Devon Pub Walks (8-18km)
Really short walks – north Devon (3-5km)
Really short walks – south Devon (3-5km)
Shortish walks in East Devon (6-8km)
Shortish walks – north Devon (6-8km)
Shortish walks – south Devon coast (6-8km)
Shortish walks – Torbay and Dartmouth (6-8km)

Exmoor Pub Walks (8-15km)
Shortish walks on Exmoor (6-9km)
Shortish walks – Quantocks and Mendips (6-8km)
Shortish walks – the Levels and south Somerset (6-8km)

Really short walks – north Cornwall (3-5km)
Shortish walks near the Land's End (6-8km)
Shortish walks on and around The Lizard (6-8km)
Shortish walks – Bodmin Moor (6-8km)
Shortish walks – north Cornwall (6-8km)
Shortish walks – St Ives to Padstow (6-8km)
Shortish walks – Truro to Looe (4-9km)